CAMERA OBSCURA

Selected works by Seán Street

Poetry
Earth and Sky (Chapbook)
Figure in a Landscape
Carvings
A Walk in Winter
This True Making
Radio and Other Poems
Radio Waves: Poems Celebrating the Wireless (ed)
Time Between Tides: New and Selected Poems 1981-2009
Cello
Jazz Time (Chapbook)

Prose
The Wreck of the Deutschland
The Bournemouth Symphony Orchestra (with Raymond Carpenter)
A Remembered Land
The Dymock Poets (new edition, 2014)
Concise History of British Radio 1922-2002
Historical Dictionary of British Radio (2nd ed.2015)
Crossing the Ether: Pre-War Public Service Radio and Commercial Competition in the UK
The Poetry of Radio – The Colour of Sound
The Memory of Sound – Preserving the Sonic Past

Stage Plays
A Shepherd's Life
Wessex Days
Honest John
Beyond Paradise

Radio Drama
The Drift of Time
Procession to the Private Sector (after David Gascoyne)

Musical Works
The Winter Bird   The Benjamin Dream   Papa Panov's Christmas
The Treasure Trail   The Pied Piper of Hamelin
(with Douglas Coombes)
Shipping Forecast   Theatre of Tango   Seventy Degrees Below Zero
(with Cecilia McDowall)

Seán Street

Camera Obscura

Rockingham Press

Published in 2016 by
The Rockingham Press
11 Musley Lane,
Ware, Herts SG12 7EN
www.rockinghampress.com

Copyright © Seán Street, 2016

The right of Seán Street to be identified as the author of this work
has been asserted by him in accordance with Section 77 of the
Copyright, Designs
and Patents Act 1988

British Library Cataloguing-in-Publication Data

A catalogue record for this book
is available from the British Library

ISBN 978-1-904851-65-3

To David Perman

Acknowledgements

'Angels on Radar' was written for the song cycle, *Flights of Angels* by Cecilia McDowall, and premiered at the 2015 Presteigne Festival by Gillian Keith (soprano) accompanied by Timothy End (piano). 'Conversation with a Chiltern Muntjac' was inspired by a passage in Richard Mabey's book, *Nature Cure*. The version of 'Elias of Dereham' included here evolved from a film script commissioned by Salisbury Cathedral and produced by Red Balloon Productions in 2015. Thanks to producer Stephanie Farmer and director Trevor Hearing.

Versions of some other poems were first published in *Acumen, Agenda, Envoi, The Manhattan Review, Rising, Salzburg Poetry Review, Sarasvati, Scintilla* and *Tears in the Fence*. 'Bournemouth' and 'Hearing Buddy Bolden' were first published in *Jazz Time* (Lapwing Publications). My thanks to Jemma Street for granting permission for her painting, *Resonance*, to be reproduced on the cover of this book, and to Nick Buchanan for photography and design.

As always, love and thanks to Jo.

Seán Street

Contents

I

The Art of Falling Slowly	11
Richard Jefferies on the Diving Board	12
Conversation with a Chiltern Muntjac	13
Suburbs	14
Old Glass	15
City Girl	16
Aconite	17
Fieldfares	18
Toad's Mouth	19
Audubon	20
Penance for Shanawdithit	21
The Last Tarpan	22

II

Short Wave	24
The Catastrophe Tapes	25
On a Line Written by Rupert Brooke	27
Reel-to-Reel	28
To the Star and Back	29
Home Delivery	30
Great Village, 1953	31
The Cathedral Church of St Brigid	32
Angels on Radar	33
Elias of Dereham	34
Matins	36
On the Air	37

III

The Calderstones — 39

IV

Camera Obscura — 45
Lesson — 46
Sun Dog — 47
How the Universe Unfolds — 48
Villanelle on Lines by Sir Thomas Wyatt — 49
A Wedding Ring — 50
Live Rails — 51
Bournemouth — 52
Morning News — 53
Trick — 54
Municipal Park — 54
The Dark at the Top of the Stairs — 55

V

The Ninth Symphony — 57
Mass in e-flat Minor — 58
Ghost Variations — 62
Windflower — 64
Manuel Venegas — 65
a-minor — 67
Music Radio — 68
Poem for Wilko Johnson — 69

Hearing Buddy Bolden			70
Sunday at the Village Vanguard			71
Twelve Bars			
	i	Twelve Bars	72
	ii	Bottleneck	72
	iii	*A Fool for You*	73
	iv	Crossroads	74
	v	*Black Cadillac Blues*	74
	vi	Mystery Train	75
	vii	*Smokestack Lightning*	76
	viii	Sonny Boy Williamson II	76
	ix	*Live at The Regal*	77
	x	*Winterreise* – Blind Lemon Jefferso*n*	78
	xi	*Backwater Blues* – Bessie Smith	78
	xii	Resolution	79
Shellac			80

I

The Art of Falling Slowly

is not easily acquired. It's all
about observing,
the closer I come the less I see.

Desiring it as trees strive towards
dancing, our flying
shapes these descending variations,

confusing more detail all the time
in a picture frame
that gets faster as it gets bigger.

It's a presumption, to be bird,
to be angel, sky
concealing the lost avian dream.

In the end as I reach out for it,
it's a nothingness
blurring to black and then exploding.

No such thing as a fixed horizon,
but the grace of light
held for a moment, the art of it.

Léo Valentin, bird-man, died Liverpool, May, 1956

Richard Jefferies on the Diving Board
Coate, Wiltshire

By 1935, the Art Deco board at Coate Water provided a nationally renowned platform for diving competitions. It is now listed.

It's an idyll bequeathed to an edge land,
derelict for years, but the ducks love it.
Swindon, if it remembers, Sundays out
here until the dusk makes it depressing.

Time to bed off if you're of the feathered
persuasion, though the M4 never sleeps.
Through years they've learnt to live with that,
far worse is the bearded ghost that troubles

them on full moon nights, him glancing around,
then on impulse executing a perfect
backwards dive, three point five somersaults in
the pike position. Bevis applauding.

Conversation with a Chiltern Muntjac
After Richard Mabey

We name but we can never know.
Bracken stirs. Curiosity –
a particular selfness

but I do not know what this is.
Move, react, freeze. Nerve and sense,
sound, smell of rut, dung, fear, rain.

We look for a definition

but I do not know what that is.
Nothing is made from an idea.
We can't exchange consciousness.
You name according to your own
bracken...

    ...that's to say history.
Move, stand, listen. Nerve and sense,
sound, smell of water, air, heat.

You name but can only guess at
suchness in others beyond you.

You can never know what that is.

Neither do I know what this is.

Suburbs

i
First light. The illusion
of wind-blown transparent
hopes drying on our lines
until the greenness hardens.

ii
In riverside kite parks
our children swing on strings
connecting them to sky.
The grass leads dogs by the nose.

iii
Mists' kiss and a fogged mind
hiding the trees' striptease
prelude to brittle bones
snapping under a hoar frost.

iv
Edging the curtains back,
listening for the song
Easter windows sing, wild
to twitch the lace blinds again.

Old Glass

An old glass window
photographing the garden
for our temporary eyes,
crown blown, and spun by a hand
two centuries gone.

An ancient picture
flexed by encounters with rain,
weathered inside by breath's mist,
the passing witness of sight,
the room's patina

and the lights' flicker.
But this flecked negative can't
print laughter's glance, sorrow's glaze
or a head's turn, for all the long
days pour through it

deep into shadows,
the street lights' probe, nights sharing
dark with every lived life lost.
For all it's a wise lens, it can't
recall the dead.

Like us it's fragile,
'though it survives time better.
Searching for coming seasons,
every morning's bottled light
awakes with ours.

Old glass out-staring
trees, cloud images' rushing
time-exposed blur. A stoic
servant, on good days it cheers
us, rainbows walls.

City Girl

You never cared for the countryside.
Walking fields has held few charms for you,
but we've come together through changing
weathers of landscapes, and you in spite
of yourself so often naming them,
that between us after all this time
we can still find the right word when they
startle us back to one another.

Aconite

It's a struggle to open
but on some days light agrees
with the season and that helps
persuade me.

Today I might just exist
in my own right. While before
there wasn't colour, now sky
reflects it.

Loam slept dark in disbelief
at this enhancement the child
became out of frailty,
bright braggart.

Things mitigate against life,
a poem flutters birthing.
You make it this time. There's no
guarantee.

Fieldfares
Anne Cluysenaar, November, 2014

It's a misnomer when we call them small hours,
an interminable place to live, bringing back
the sleepless absolute of things we'll never mend.
Nothing for it, just listen to north-easterlies'
all-night storm broadcasts transmitted from the Baltic.

But to see through eventual dawn those sudden
birds dissolve across the garden – the morning's gift of it –
is to encounter a definition of you
in what we might have shared: 'Look, Fieldfares, we've Fieldfares!'
as they shoal round, leafing winter trees' antennae.

They've flown towards us for millennia of miles,
even after that, profligate in their circling,
exhausting our space, one wing for all, filling air
harbours with verticity while somewhere emptied
past summers echo their departure's bereavement.

There are things, Keats wrote to Bailey, require greetings
of the spirit to give them existence, fleeting
engagements in thin places, advent transmissions,
consecrations in skies, clouds. And understanding
this migrant flight, searching the winds for a presence.

Toad's Mouth
A6187, Burbage Bridge, Derbyshire, February, 1959

Revising a childhood's Hathersage road
from Fox House, twisting through rubble
of earth's bone cutting a crackling edge on sky,
memory goes where gritstone and shale take it
towards Snake, with Sheffield echoing behind,
ahead, recollected cartography of loaded names
in a misted fictioned distance out somewhere beyond
Hope, Blue John's gleam, Mam Tor's murmured mourning
for Ashopton and Derwent's perpetual drowning,
and my music from another world dying
as it first rang, American guitars' soundtrack
to a car's television window on Place,
dread watching for the Toad Rock's stare,
the shock confirming where mind's eye had it placed.

Suddenly now a corner too dangerous
to contemplate, and a dark stone crawls again
from failing light, a source proven, snared grey
in a headlight. So this at least was true.
More lizard than toad though, the head
of something emerging out of the moor,
a tight-lipped face tilted at sky,
a sidelong look holding its council
and opinion, sitting in judgement now
as then, a monstrous certainty
and the shape of unchangeable fact
surrounded by fallible hindsight, touched alive
like a remembered song. Time turns its corner,
Toad stares from his, too dangerous to contemplate.

Audubon
January 1851

The Robin said I sang you your first
song on ragged shores, across the chill
of your fearful premonitions.

The Crow said I weep for you,
chronicler who saw through my terror
the antipathy of strangers.

The Shearwater said together
we mourn a black cloud ascending,
then rushing down like a torrent.

Seabirds with human voices,
the tiny lost cries of final
interacting things. I can't hear

yesterday but messages from stars
alien as a gull's eye
in dark spaces brush me,

stumbling through broken stones,
trying to find a way out
of these ruins' stillness.

The Double-Crested Cormorant said
I mourn you from my cold sky
and granite cliffs, bleak waters.

The Arctic Tern said I danced
through the air above and around you
while you froze my grace in these winds.

You have passed like us
over many a league of ocean.
We mourn you on your solitary isle.

Penance for Shanawdithit
Widely believed to have been the last of the native Beothuk people of Newfoundland, Shanawdithit died of tuberculosis on 6 June 1829 in St. John's. She was 28.

Fishers clustering in Random Sound.
This boy's from the Homeland, meaning me,
a long way to swim. The Beothuk
might have said that but they didn't,
gave beads and accepted invasion,
occupation, infection, and look,
we're back in Eden at the cast out.
New worlds are always to be taken,
are they not? A philosophical
concept, belonging, rather like home.
But it's the world that's truly foreign,
snow crabs scuttling in the deep cold, squid
swarming through the sting of sea-flowers
floating, blossoming on dark water.

There's no atonement once peoples die –
no price to pay, what's to barter with now?
We may tenant a landscape but we
never own land. So what would you have
me do? Fall on the tide from that cliff,
swallowed by indifferent sea,
to surface, far as the night comes on,
beyond help, beyond granite and berg,
until awestruck jiggers see only
my seal-head sacrifice in giant
deeps, swimming away from history's
long pointing witness? I could do that.
It wouldn't bring her back, nor stop it
happening again. But I'd drown pure.

The Last Tarpan

*In 1879, pursued by humans, the last wild, pure Tarpan mare
ran off the edge of a crevasse in Ukraine and died*

Paint me on cave walls,
you'll not own me, you
caught in your earth. Last
of my kind I'll fly,
choosing to be more
than meat,
 choosing air
racing into space
rather than be flesh
in caves. Pursuing
me you can only
drive me to this dance.

I choose to arc off
the edge of the world,
choose empowerment
to make me mythic,
perfect memory
of wind in a mane,
to be Pegasus.

II

Short Wave

Tuning the endless white noise.
Interminable. One faint
voice after another.   Mixed
audio detritus came
and went, discarded, dialled
out of mind as the needle's
searchlight moved on, pausing when
a pitch or a tone cut through,
tricking the ear to engage
as an eye deceives itself.

A shout or prayer, a cry
like a hand lifted for help,
calling out in the dark, drowned
in the boredom of seeking,
(always excused with hindsight,
just too quiet to notice,
as we might convince ourselves
a trick of the light perhaps,
it's easy to miss these things.)
The forgiveness of ourselves,
amnesia of conscience
hides us from what we are.

In the end, I don't recall,
for all the weary scanning,
if we ever found anything
worth attending to at all.

Ears hear but a mind listens,
and as Thoreau said, *it's not*
what you look at that matters,
it's what you see. (Or choose to.)

The Catastrophe Tapes
Towton, 29 March 1461

Last words and old technology,
recordings made at unknown speeds,
unspecified sounds now all but
beyond us, speaking in strange ways.
Days gone they would have known all this,
we're learning to decipher these
distant voices, this far crying
from muffled soundscapes, a message
we can just start to interpret,
archived against a future.

Still, some sounds enlist you, make you
witness. *The budding tree by me*
in a landscape I've never walked
records my end's living moment
but you will not hear it until
the field opens beyond silence,
something else calling. To be in
space otherwise anechoic
will turn listeners mad because
here there are now dead men's voices.

Filed as 'The Catastrophe Tapes',
this is what remained when records
failed: *I wonder that one day some*
who believe ideas as we
will try to read, find the language
of a lost hand's frozen speaking
before its actions dissolved it.
(Hold this if you can, because no life
light can burn beyond this snow storm,
but surely someone will listen?)

That distant sound is coming close,
do you think it's coming closer?
it seems to me so...Who would run
before it comes? Futile the thought
of it now. (Are we holding sound?
Are you hearing any of this?
Keep it turning, it may matter
someday, they may need to know it).
Turning, it seems they saw a cloud
form, then there's a sort of white noise.

High pitched screams sounding like feedback,
panic compounded by decay,
distortion, meaningless chaos,
we returned to the same problems,
frequency or sound quality
or both, things we've not managed to
read, incompatibility
of formats, tantalising, strange;
we could have learned more from all this,
but it remains work in progress.

On a Line Written by Rupert Brooke

Knowing with hindsight is such a sweet and easy thing.
What would you have said if before death you'd seen the fact
of what the others saw? Given half a chance to sing,
what sort of sonnet would you have crafted out of that?
Would you have chronicled – left in no man's land to cope
under flares – the terror's sound that had retched in dug-out
dreams, would you have wept, wide blind-eyed, at the thought of hope?
If he'd lived, what would The Soldier have talked about?

And what would you have said, if you had known
the endlessness of it all, seen the furthest reaches
of vested interests turn your swimmers' cleanness sour
to justify a war. What then would have been your tone?
Would you, seeing babies washed up on foreign beaches,
still say *Now God be thanked, who has matched us with His hour*?

Reel-to-Reel

Playback gets harder as the years go on.
Hearing your voice silent, as memory,
is one thing but the sound of it moving
across time as old technology turns
in your once lived-in space is something else.

Suddenly you're here, those familiar
tones, recognised normality taken
for granted in the forgotten daily
grainstore of what made your spirit visceral,
circumventing the tape's oxide witness.

Old wallpaper bleeds through, the place wrapping
itself once more round the time between words,
the clock's tick, beyond it the field you knew,
hanging from the far side, the steam train's hoot
transmitting across mist through summer's rain.

Walls have heard it all before and the tape's
off-switch records itself in the stillness
after you close this last door. A pause and then
involuntary important things
shout, drowning out your whispered documents.

To the Star and Back
Henry Vaughan

Galaxies over Mersey. I tune in.
The compass giddies, looks for him due south.

What ever 'tis, whose beauty here below
Attracts thee thus and makes thee stream and flow...

His immense idea, the sentience
of trees, stones, what a star might know of it.

I wait for return signals in the dark,
the airwaves crackling with activity –

full of plants, rocks, planets – listen across
Dee, Moel Famau down to Usk, then loud, clear:

These are the magnets which so strongly move
And work all night upon thy light and love.

Home Delivery
Dr. P. Aaron Potter visits Culbone Farm, October, 1797

Someone needed to bring the package round
or else who knows if the muse would have called
at all. Allow four days, the chemist said,
so the fault may well have been with yourself.
By line thirty-six you were out of steam

anyway – let's not blame the health service.
Yes, it was quite bad timing, but then there's
always some sabotaging Geraldine
to spray grey paint on the moment, shrivel
a great thought like death clenching a spider.

That said, sometimes you just run dry of it,
drugs, drink, inspiration. Write high, edit
low, to misquote what Hemingway never
said. Clearly that wasn't an option here.
Whatever, the door will do as a scapegoat.

I'm not the first by any means – won't be
the last — to knock on your coffin searching
for the *Marie Celeste* of poetry,
meanwhile waiting all day long, hoping for
the bell that announces my prescription.

Great Village, 1953
Elizabeth Bishop, Nova Scotia

Here's a new way of looking at an old sky,
trunk road arcing past a cornered spire,
pausing at a white cottage, and history
where hindsight takes curated soundings higher
into a reality resumed and turned
to celebration, suddenly graceful.
Time shaping a long hurt through memory earned,
the form of past tenses' phenomena, full
of liquid air and the disappearing word,
moment's invisibility and the hand
that heard it. Then the cry of a dreadful bird
projected by a dreamed recollection and
the bruise on a blank page, again and again
soaking earth like this morning's complicit rain.

The Cathedral Church of St. Brigid
(Kildare)

Pagan plains leak in.
We crush them silent, arches
braced to hold heaven.

Dolmens had their day
some several gods ago.
We've found the true one.

Pray for us sinners.
There's the thrush singing again.
Focus on the Host.

Angels on Radar

We understood the early
warnings of war - not these ghosts.
Caught here was something mythic,
echoes out at sea, spirits
along coastlines following
weather fronts that showed nothing
for all we scrambled and searched,
and so we called them angels.

Their haunting was a healing,
horizon's visitations,
angelic murmurations,
for what are angels but birds -
lapwing, starling and fieldfare -
what are these birds but angels
bringing shape, song to the need
in our searching, a blessing.

Elias of Dereham

*'Master Elias of Dereham' (1167-1246) was present
at the sealing of Magna Carta. He was a church mason
and designer who supervised the building of Salisbury Cathedral.*

Data per manum nostram.

Winds across the Plain, down from Sarum,
stone on sand, sheep in the valley,
winds swaying the spire.

Before we made the stone dance
we made the word stone.

But it's fragile, this stone
as sheepskin parchment,
strong and fragile as truths
inscribed in the heart (which is fragile),
speaking thought, freedom

born in the clamour
of necessity, the crash,
shout and build of requirement
against tyranny, scribed here
to express what we stand for.

As spire's fragile aspiration
strives up from bulk
to the invisible,
so do Time's winds transport
transparent freedoms,
flexing like stone towers to move
in wind's change, making
a new shape of it, being constant.

I, Master Elias, send greeting.
I who carved stone
saw the constitution of hope,
I among first witnesses touched
the Great Charter, present to hear
the King's teeth grind,
the sound of rage on his own stone.

Elias the mason, and the words
on sheepskin, borne by me to this place,
growing through change, challenge, insistence
to the very thing you are now.
Just as you are, so was I,
just as these truths are now.

Winds across the Plain,
down from Veretes Sarisberi,
stone on sand, sheep in the valley,
storm swaying the spire.

I was there when it was said and written.
I, canon in this place by the Grace of God
was here, saw the birthing of fragile stone,
the fragile idea made stone,
brought to this place the fragile idea.

Data per manum nostram.

Matins
(Berwick-upon-Tweed Ramparts)

Familiar light, known music.
This is what we should be working
towards, unbroken silence.

We begin as a bell does, struck
at another's will into sound.
Light emerges from silence.

Because of where we are, a frame
of time holds it. Light and a bell
know better, their place in things.

As a bell moves away towards
betterment from its literal
blow, as dark moves back to light,

physical to transparent,
so then should we, so we might.

On the Air

Too much bone and blood to go far.
body is too dense, against the law
of what we came from, what we become.
What it would be to be air,

a pure radio of clear air
and to know it, ether for apports,
things flung across light, broadcasting seed,
instants gifted from elsewhere

through atmosphere, their silverness
sensed in momentary transmissions
before transcendence can be explained
by our heavy receivers.

III

The Calderstones

In a suburban park of the same name in south Liverpool stand the six Calderstones, profusely decorated with rock art symbols and believed to have been once part of a burial chamber used by a Neolithic community up to 3,000 years BC.

1

Distant thunder over the park,
but here's a baby's perfect sleep
beside me in a cupped stillness
that dares itself to be broken.

I listen to a bell fading,
the physical shout of a strike
made before a pyramid found
shape, down to a hum, but singing.

*Space between trees making a room
to fill with our living and dead.
Here we have made us a clearing
with stones for their veneration.*

*Cut meaning in sandstone, leave here
expiation in spiral, arc,
our footprint, shape of a species.
We are moving from flesh to air.*

*We gouge and cut, sharpen, funnel
the fire to air. Our buried dead
tease bewilderment with these shapes,
etch each of us a message here.*

*We gather, circle, sending dead
forward, filling rooms with burnt bones,*

*smoke above trees transmitting their
spirals, and air becomes their dance.*

*Squat, then shape, cut bone, staring
 out across waters, tracks across
marshlands below the hill, eyes on
the hill fort south, smoke from mountains.*

Before a stone henge ringed itself
aligned to solstice or white horse
cut across sward, this death was new,
red rock standing on tumuli.

They leave fragments of their dumb dead
too distant to be ghosts, only
implied presences and signified
by a scattering, scattered by

winds' broadcast through millennia.
What was it you had hoped to find?
Kin? Sense of solidarity?
Only that we seeds all vanish.

We're presences carved year on year,
sound from silence, the two of us
listening to the almost heard,
what menhir calls to child and man.

We both came through forgotten
whispers to this pause between speech,
and weathering of languages
melts memory's too-soft sandstone.

Dormitory prehistory –

if pressed before recollection,
what but lore could reference
inherited dust of past lives?

Marsh hardened to a dock. The ships
come and go, come and go, are gone
in the time a feather flutters,
gone before it touches the ground.

Jewel, bone, axe and spear buried
against Time, burnt broken bone snared
then lost, the stones' cut eroded,
covered, earth stopping every mouth.

But decode spiral and footprint, make them
narrative, language, present-tense
them to retrieve, cut, shape and voice
a clearing. All space holds echoes.

2

The park in autumn. Dim thunder,
a child on a swing and arcing
like a pendulum, the red stones
grouped in shadow and safely parked.

Six stones left, but you would know
the place beyond its thickened air.
We have cleared, lost and retrieved, made
rooms in suburban verdancy.

We have left you the grunt of stone
as witness. Sometimes I have thought

*I heard sounds from the river, moving
through the marsh, spirits I watched for,*

*but they did not come. Perhaps you
were here? Against your coming, I
waited. Though watching for long,
still you did not come. I have lived long*

*but I cannot live much longer,
meantime I bury our dead here
and the red stone crowns them. More, more
they leave, and now I am alone.*

Truth is, we're all solitaries
by Calderstones, burying dead,
sharing our time with shattered graves
talking to us, not listening.

The walls fall and tenements rise,
bombs fall, children dance and are gone
all in the curved air of a swing.
Marsh, dock, park. All is always now.

A clock ticks once, a child's swing arcs,
each describing a millennium.
She rises to sky. By the time
she descends I will be long gone,

park and suburb, city all gone,
only the light across water
to far mountains, cry of seabirds.
I watched for you – you did not come.

We come too late for those who watched
for us. They leave before we reach
them. Just relics, remembrances,
a mortal's votive detritus.

But seventy hands shaken will make
five millennia quickly bridged,
the movement of flesh into air,
air into flesh across lifetimes.

All space holds echoes. A clearing
in woodland, a circle of stones,
shaped spirals into cups of sound,
the tense of them always present,

heard in stillness, spinning outwards
from the marks that a hand made then,
still here though muffled to thunder
murmuring across the city.

A seabird overflies the stones,
a feather falls slowly through air,
for five thousand years will turn, fall
iridescent, mirror's bevel

reflecting askew of daylight
something oblique in the corner
of Time's eye, and accidents that
give presences to history.

A bell fades past the child in me,
while a strike on stone ringing from
before little but the stars had
a shape, though to a hum, still sings.

IV

Camera Obscura
For my Granddaughter, Autumn 2014

Clouds have done their late reveal New Moon, but I don't have glass
powerful enough to focus you in harvest time,
and I suspect I'll be increasingly enveloped in
the fog smother that descends on all receding seasons.

Still, universe is not too dark for light-years' likenesses,
flickers from Andromeda's snapping paparazzi,
so let's strike a pose – if there's anything to print us sharp
as the clocks go back, then the flash from a galaxy might.

A cosmic camera, you and I caught on film, laughing
for the sky through a memory's telephoto lens,
and if its shutter clicked now across all that milky space,
past and future might yet hold hands, archived in new moonlight.

Lesson

The universe starts at our feet.
This simple realisation
should strike early rather than late,
before we are old and replete
and tired of aspiration.

Sun Dog
Parhelia foretell stormy weather – Aratus.

Night's a rush when the weather fronts accelerate
then pause between changes from one ninth wave's track
to another, gusting in squalls from sea's state
beyond horizons, driving the current back.

Extract hope from expectation, a hard psalter's
shouting through walls, forcing flood and storm's breaking
songs from rainbow fragments' oracle altar,
god of barometers tracking and chasing

us down. One hung deceiving pastels that day
over the ebb before the salt came surging
through chopped water leaving the ghosts holding sway
in the Dante hours with all tides converging.

Sleepless to see what sky was forewarning,
what the waters savaged, nothing I suspect
compares with what's overtaken the morning.
We build our frail defences in retrospect.

How the Universe Unfolds

A morning through the side window,
empty sky, then a brief shadow
thought as if by someone coming
up the moss brick path to the door.

A gull over rooftops freewheeled
right to left, then disappeared down
while making its temporal shapes,
a glide, moving but motionless.

A fly on the arm of the chair,
the oil of its wing catching light
out of season with its shadow
on the surface of a second.

A postman hooded for winter.
The mail that day brought one letter.
Pushed onto the porch floor, it was
creased, rained-on, only slightly torn.

Villanelle on Lines by Sir Thomas Wyatt
(1503-1542)
Anne Williams, Hillsborough campaigner, died 18 April 2013

My sweet, alas, forget me not,
I'm the long conscience that seeks out what you are,
although daily ye see me not.

How is it with you? Have you yet
not understood the awakened hurt I share?
My sweet, alas, forget me not.

In fact it was ever my lot
to pursue you. I am always so, so near
although daily ye see me not.

Just remember what you forgot
and when you remember you will catch my stare.
My sweet, alas, forget me not.

When you killed my trust, oh then what
did we come to? I am pain's day and hope's star,
although daily ye see me not.

Truth will pursue you, be it cold or hot,
even though it seems to you you've come so far.
My sweet, alas, forget me not,
although daily ye see me not.

A Wedding Ring

The love in the ring surrounded him
until one evening it started to bite
under its gold. The long vow's weight of it
tightened on his finger, drawing its blood,
refusing to relinquish promises.

It fought him hard for his freedom, a hand
losing a life, space on skin confessing
an ending by sacrificing shared time
to a blank exposed place, turning death-white
as the long-denied light started its heal.

Begun in the night and accomplished
at dawn, at last the loving ring released
him from the wedding day in it, grew cold.
He sat and held it gently as it died,
as its voice whispered, gasped and then vanished.

Live Rails

Terminus ghosts are back, early
Southern Railways forest green electric
trains always silently leaving,
gliding children away from the final
faces of family too close
to their dying to ever see again.

The ache in the throat at waving
them off, although they seemed to be staying,
memory holding their picture,
diminishing until north tactfully
erased it in smoke, change by change.
So how were they? Pretending, *they seemed fine.*

Brave-smiled, separated by blurred
glass, held signals, already beyond touch,
afraid of what eye contact might
betray in public, the words left unsaid,
there must have always been machines
like this to inform our mortality.

All goodbyes transform the present,
history finalised by a door-close.
Today your smooth pendolino,
poised to fulfil its function, pauses, then
accelerates imperceptibly
south through irrevocable stations.

Bournemouth
The Nearness of You

Things took longer, radios warming up,
coal-gas cooking, building a family,
but ageing was something they did faster
till the out-of-season town where so much
had been promised on holiday grew still,
remembering it, three roads from the sea.

Here's where they came, young, before the children,
year on year, away from smoke, community,
each summer, far from work, routine and roots
in the sunshine time, this is what they wished
themselves – Lionel Hampton at the Winter
Gardens – and their 1953 song.

A life's wavebands in a medicated
room waited by the phone, and when he called,
broadcasting family news from outside
the archive of her memory, it came
from a strange place, this duty done, asking
after her, not really wanting to know,

not really wanting to hear stories told
too many times, or guess why she grew sad
hearing *The Nearness of You*, retrieving
the presence of his father's voice, reborn,
re-recording her recollection's sound,
longing for some sort of shared experience.

Somewhere high above and beyond coastlines,
beyond the Earth's curve where transmissions grow
lonely and faint but can't die, what we were
flickers, searches in vain for receivers,
sends out messages with no one at all
listening, or for that matter caring.

Morning News

Dark. A truck dopplers bass outside
then the road's on its own again.
Pause. Rain. Tarmac gets a voice, sings
white noise under a clubber's thump
but like all radio language
it disappears. The phone. No one
ever calls at this time. Boards creak.
Weather tries to decide. Boards creak.
Curtains. There's the sky, up early.

Trick

I've never quite understood how you did that.
Even now, thinking it through, rehearsing it,
I still can't fathom out the sheer sleight of hand.
Perhaps I looked away for a split-second,
or maybe it was that a light flashed beyond
you, dazzling me. I was sure I could solve it,
willing the whole act to make some sort of sense,
so determined not to let you get away
with it. But you won before my very eyes,
left me reaching for the space where once you were.

Municipal Park

An empty wooded room
with a capacity
for silence, common land
turned Quaker,
finding the white of quiet
when the council's birds stopped
and stillness formed a circle.

The Dark at the Top of the Stairs

At night you could feel it spreading,
occupying the top-floor rooms,
ignoring the fleet urgencies
downstairs as doors opened and closed
on things that seemed to matter
to those who opened and closed doors.

Risers, treaders separated
worlds, ascent to invisible
space, soundless dark staring, a blank
in the ancient house chorus
of noise where boards creaked, doors opened
and closed, and the landing waited.

And it grew, oozed across floorboards,
this contagion of emptiness
listening to the bright voices,
never ever once answering,
recording without prejudice,
moving through the upstairs rooms

as all the doors opened and closed
and the old house shifted as it
sluiced to and fro above our heads.
Oh, it took time, understanding
the silence where staircases end,
 what's left behind, what each night brings.

V

The Ninth Symphony

can be a creative staging post, then again
quite possibly an ultimate destination,
a self-penned though unintentional resignation
(as with Mahler, Bruckner, Schubert and Beethoven).
It may be good to clear the desk, but in the end
we don't plan them to be our final finales,
would rather accrue for further biennales
in the hope there'll be time for something more to send.
Years have always been rivers to cross, but bridges
are longer and less well built than they used to be,
and our departure is never a guarantee
of arrival, whatever the contract pledges.
Work on the basis that the whole sad thing's a bluff,
and let circumstance decide when enough's enough.

Mass in e-flat major
after Schubert, 1828

i Kyrie

Steps leading down into a black water.
The needle starts its probe, spiking tissue
and the invasion asks its own questions.
I can no longer guess where matter ends
and spirit begins, the invisible
obscured by the physical, the thinking
concealed by the pain which is its mercy.

ii Gloria
Nant Gwrtheyrn

Water's edge then dark beyond us.
The words say one thing but the way
we say them is what reveals things.
The companionship of daylight,
that is enough to pray for now
and it is somewhere far out there,
celebration of consciousness,
stones weathering storm then storm
before our bones reach their morning.

So you can see when that light stings
the cold it is the deep distance
that awes, defeats through unfathomed
space. You cannot help but wonder
now, faced with the pockets of blood
we are, nothing better to show
the truth of the ordinary,
the honesty of a morning
than empty skies.

        What is there? Swim
until currents win. Little left
to be achieved, everything
to be attempted. Everything.

iii Credo

One by one metal shutters,
gridlocks in evening rain
stop the city in the act
of heading out from the week
to material churches.

Pilgrims, it is the journey
and you are what you believe,
and what we believe comes to us
from an inventory we
make, patterns and acts of faith,
like trusting light to wake us.

Between prayer and promise
there is an uncertain light.

iv Sanctus

The angels are accountable to sacred rules,
but I live as best I can in silence as thick
as fog, and still not understanding the purpose.
Pleni sunt coeli et terra gloria tua.
A memory then, to consecrate the places
that knew us, uncovering the layers under
new tides before the mind's pictures start to dissolve.

v Benedictus
Coastal Erosion, Formby Point

The next high water claims back
what we called our own. Nothing
belongs and we own nothing,
what eats into us now made
us, and so we have no cause
for complaint. That said, what eats
us is our sad envy of
unlived days, but I have seen
my children grow, so I have
no cause, no cause for complaint.

Sands give way under our feet,
a far rig's fire bleeds into
dark, the wind farm's choir tenses
for vespers and wings beat down
over me, heading inland.
Benedictus qui venit,
the airborne ice sends spirits
homeward. I flicker and fade.

vi Agnus Dei

The air is full of textings
and a shrill plastic panic,
full of prayers and promise.
Have mercy on us. We seek
a permanent present, so
there's comfort in removing
history to make ourselves
eternally immediate.

This is close to accomplishment,
the sacred almost erased
by routine.

           In my moment
I would wish to be somehow
a continuing partner
to the world and its selfness
with me, but nothing belongs.

I try to guess where matter
ends, where the spirit begins,
acts of faith, like trusting
the unheard and unclimbed,
the idea of Place,
love when it's shared, unseen,
existing notwithstanding.

Ghost Variations
During the night of 17 February 1854 Robert Schumann wrote a theme 'dictated by the angels'.

A piano holding its breath in the darkness.
A murmur from behind a door, rushing water
on stone, the heard memory of a voice singing
beyond a river obscuring all but the next
room's song. There is no one, no one in the next room,
so a voice is all I have, drowning in distance.

It's the journey inside me makes this a distance
such that now I can barely see through the darkness
towards the door beyond which there's music, a room
and the rushing of the river's noise, its water
moving me note by note on to what happens next,
making memory of a piano's singing.

Variations. Call and response. A voice singing
something new and perfect but heard from a distance
and recalled between one interval and the next,
known silently, as real as all else the darkness
brings through demonic whispers, the rustle water
drowns between me and dictation from the far room.

A piano playing softly in the next room.
Through the held breath of fog in my head there's singing.
I document the moment, music as water
moving downstream, passing, shifting to far distance
as time comes, passes and moves on from one darkness
to another, into whatever happens next.

Note by note, the inevitable in what's next
between where I am and the strange haunted room
that teaches me, the murmuring sound of darkness,
stillness my last chance, the sinking of singing
in the white noise of a river closing distance

across time, hope turned to the music of water.

I now understand the kinship of song and water.
I was on the other side of what happened next
when I began to feel the nearness and distance
of voices pushing together inside my room,
but I never knew it was my own ghost singing,
the ghost of who I once was, somewhere in darkness.

There was the noise of water obscuring the room
before what happened next, the end of all singing,
voices drowned by distance, song blinded by darkness.

Windflower
(Edward Elgar to Alice Stuart-Wortley, 1911)

I saw snows linger above springtime, then
I sensed that these days will not come again
Windflower, and we shall all be ghosts soon,
shadows in shadows between stars, this pen
etching dark that moves through the garden's noon.

Whatever happens to the certainty,
we could ask no more of things than to be
daughters of the wind when snows melt, aligned
to an inherited transparency,
colour remembered, something of that kind.

Manuel Venegas

Vienna. In 1897 the composer Hugo Wolf slipped into syphilitic insanity, leaving sixty pages of an unfinished opera.

There. There was a sound then, the glow
it created when it sang aloud
from its mad lantern, from autumn
born into encounters between
rhythms unencumbered with old
meanings, the reflection of roads
against low cloud making place shine,
the torches that these voices light.

A sound map of a known city
which is ourselves, as it happens,
change and the rain on pavements heard
from fiakers or in shelters,
it may be like caves. Memory
in its instant, ideas in
what rings on walls, music being
time made orphic as it happens.

Scraps only, piece by piece making
something, a lifetime, a poem,
scraps of torn paper enlisting
what? An idea to shape something
of themselves, rejection's thunder
fisted to nothing, while I fade,
am fading from living to past
dead, something perhaps history.

Then when I pushed a door open,
went in, there was the music swept
into corners, bare boards, white peeled
walls and pale light from the dawn street.
I noticed trapped notes making good

their escape, passing me in ones
and twos, scurrying down the hall
stairs, always just out of my reach.

Hum of the blood, beat of the heart,
pathways through woods from street glitter
marked out by these footsteps falling,
iambics of walking alone.
I turned away from the huddle
cliquing each other about self,
found a home again in empty
rooms, the echo of unborn floors.

a-minor

If you came back as sound it would
be a low dark note in this room,
this front parlour with a piano,
ferns, your books over there, you held
in the act of rising from your chair,

a primeval voice as you guessed
what they were here to say, the hall
outside, the door's glass opening
onto a path, lawn and privet,
a gate past which the normal still

remains unfrozen, layers
of time concealing the witness
of it, missing the memory
of you here, but the piano
holding an echo through the years.

Strings still vibrate, the soundboard hums.
Everyone's throat has its own sob, but
the primal lives somewhere outside
time, will come to each one of us
and we'll know it when we hear it,

something of ourselves belonging
to winds through the peaks of pines' harp
in a forest, a song so bleak
as to be beyond animal,
the start and ending of all sound.

Music Radio

Each our own offshore station,
lights across tides in the darkness,
and the broadcasts calling back
transmissions from before the clocks
drowned out every pre-set network.

Songs last even if the signal
fails, just as long as memory
continues to chase the slow fade,
so tune in. How can you remember
things if you don't forget them first?

The fact is it's all still there, sound,
always there in your radio,
recording itself and slipping
into a folder for when you
need it, backed up on the hard drive.

Want a golden age? Try the one
you just recovered, your brand name's
nostalgia. Be your own history,
and make the most of it, because
tomorrow it's someone else's turn.

Poem for Wilko Johnson

I dreamed I was Wilko Johnson,
had wings and a Telecaster
and rock 'n' roll made the pain go,
and so I could write about it
without hurting too much, fed by
the blood of guitars. So it was
that music saved my life. Saved me.

A tough one to wake up from that,
but then there he was, Wilko from
Oil City singing dreams come true,
and rock 'n' roll made the pain go
with wings and a Telecaster.

Hearing Buddy Bolden

Soft walls built themselves during the night, wool
premonitions wrinkled grey like a brain.
November's silence, the school fields only
an assumption, an idea, the day
smothered in a membrane, no evidence
or symptom. We appear to be alone.

Breaking the rule of the warden trees' *hush*,
a trumpet cry just once over the rec.,
Gabriel arcing through his cathedral,
the summit of prayer or John's seven
apocalypse horns and found litany
in Buddy's stomp from another side.

Amen. Imagine then this sound borne from
ragtime by smoke and whiskey across time's
sepia through Louis, Bix and Bechet,
remade by patina in their phrasing,
informing a day's meaning, preaching
jazz by striving towards a single note.

There are some kind rooms in the blues, places
to go we can walk and control our grief,
seeing light ahead through a distant door,
out of the cramped world unfogged on a curve
rising beyond our present tense, knowing
it's a constant candle, and still calling.

Sunday at the Village Vanguard
Scott LaFaro, died July 6, 1961

It was an equal voice, partners
touching each other at harmonies
and the serendipity of minds
making a poetry, singing
while their church's moment stayed kind.
I thought that I'd imagined it,
but when I turned on memory
there was your Sunday, still playing.

The Vanguard, coming together
with Bill and Paul. Somehow it was
one single touchstone between three,
city mostly oblivious
outside, missing communion.
Time (who just can't improvise) saw
and gasped, tried to stop but couldn't.
No imagination. Jazzless.

Twelve Bars

The blues was bleeding the same blood as me.
                                      B.B. King

i
Twelve Bars

12 bars are all you'll ever need.
Mix with what the palette gives you,

any old painter man knows that –
a full glitter-ball of dance steps

or a universe of sorrows,
you can make an infinity

with just the right colour and shade,
with a seventh or a chord change.

Tune your thinking to open G,
or what you will. A frame of rhyme,

12 bars are all you need to paint
joy, pain, make a shape out of it.

ii
Bottleneck
Tampa Red: Seminole Blues, 1937

It's the steel sound that slides through your brain.
When it's doing that, that's all there is.

It's like sea wash the tides pour up dock
walls at you in winter. Like heartache,

like some sort of lightning inverted,
like a thought's intravenous coursing,

like a scream from a housing project,
like something floating at low water.

When he sang *I've got the blues so bad
it hurt my tongue to talk*, the real gist

was that now there's nothing to discuss
and we don't have words, this sound says it.

        iii
   A Fool for You
Ray Charles - Newport,1958

The stage lights sang and glittered blue, gold
moonlight across the sad park shadows.

Put your sorrow out in the air
in front of crowds and engineers.

That piano sounded like tears,
horns grieving, moaning behind him,

then at the end of it there was
his scream, a doppler shift of pain.

Seven minutes of blues as gospel
and six seconds to break your heart.

I know it must be something...that note,
there because it just had to be.

iv
Crossroads

Just to have the devil's talent
alone will never be enough,
but to sing the twelve o'clock dark
then turn into its idea,
that could be a good career move.
A half-seen shade in a corner,
history melding to fable,
now that could make something happen.
Becoming a ghost to invent
possibilities for crossroads
in the mind would be to make me
song itself, make me a poem.

v
Black Cadillac Blues
Sam Hopkins, 1912-1982

Here come Sam, all white eyes, white teeth
sittin' up there playin' guitar,

singin' the old car blues, singin'
'bout the old thunder and lightnin',

singin' 'bout what he sure do lack,
black cadillac in the mornin'.

Blues, rhythm and blues, rock 'n' roll,
sex, drugs, booze, haze across the floor,

the guitar just soundin' 'lectric
even when it's not plugged in right,

and here's Lightnin', sittin' up there,
white-wall tyres, *all white eyes, white teeth.*

vi
Mystery Train
Junior Parker, Sun Studios, 1953

The mystery's in the long black name.
Train, train, a shadow down the line
between forest firs in the snow,
an unstoppable headlong train.

Whatever it hits, it won't stop
coming down the line, down the line,
from shadows in a long dark cave
beyond the wheel-turning's flicker.

The mystery's in the journey,
and talking to shadows haunting
the long black line curving behind,
the ghosts in Sam's dark studio.

vii
Smokestack Lightning
Howlin' Wolf, 1964

Backstage memory – a giant
of a man singing it – his smile.

If your soul never dies Chester
and this is devil's music,

then curse me with you and give me
a spoonful of blues, I'll be blessed.

Now the programme you signed that night
is lost, and a disc's nowhere voice

sings *I'll never see you no more,
ah why don't ya hear me cryin'?*

but if soul never dies Chester,
curse me with you, I'll be blessed.

viii
Sonny Boy Williamson II
1964

The gent in the suit with the umbrella
and the briefcase is a grand vizier,

a menace when he's quiet, safer when
his blue harmonica's mood is talking.

His sweet smile is full of whiskey's acid,

(he'll die of Arkansas within a year.)

You gotta help me he is murmuring
to someone, *can't do it all by myself.*

Some sounds take you back to who you once were,
some sounds that once happened go on and on.

Just as he said *I'm gonna try to find
my happy home, bird I'm gone, bird I'm gone.*

ix
Live at the Regal
B.B. King, November 21, 1964

Me, Lucille, down at the Regal,
a cold windy November night,

we sang *Sweet Little Angel,* sang
Help the Poor, we sang *Please Love Me,*

and the crowd, they sang too, the crowd
called and cried and shouted and laughed,

Kenny, Bobby and Johnny blew,
Duke and Leo and Sonny gave

it rhythm and blues, and Lucille
wept in my arms and it was so cold

outside in Chicago that night,
but inside we made us a world.

x
Winterreise – **Blind Lemon Jefferson**
Lord it's one kind favor I'll ask of you,
Please see that my grave is kept clean.

At Wortham, Texas now there's
a clean cemetery in your name,

so Lemon, *it's a bad wind*
that'll never change as it's turned out.

But first there was your journey's
anonymous trudging snow blindness,

living the blues just the way
a bluesman should as your myth went off

westbound, cold from Chicago
into a dark that's even blinder.

It's a long old lane ain't got
no end. Sound's memory lives longer.

xi
Backwater Blues – Bessie Smith

The song's about the rain,
the river and the place,
about flood after flood.

Backwater's beyond song,
burnt into the hard drive,
a time's long memory

held by a disc cutter.

Sometimes you don't even
need song because the place
sings itself. At night in
the lowlands, sometimes you
drown, sometimes you're baptised.

xii

Resolution

I may make the news tomorrow,
you'll hear word of your man some day.
I may be the news tomorrow,
or there'll be word another day.
There's blood along the alleyway,
there's thunder across the bay.

Heard the radio this morning,
they said the time has come to go.
It was on the news this morning,
looks like it's time for me to go.
All things work out as they ought to,
God or the Devil wills it so.

Shellac

Coming from tactile days it seems
things go backwards as they spin out
into invisibility.
Nothing to see, nothing to touch,
no artefact to hand children
and nothing to prove an archive
exists for those of frail hearing.
At least the old technology
gave us sound as a contact sport.

Music is beyond physical,
proof of spirit's transparency,
and virtual data may be
eternal. Who knows? No limits
after all, unbreakable, smooth,
not like pre-electric days when
tones were less numeric, when you
heard a frantic song racing by –
clicking, fractured – before your ears,
the way a shellac disc was made,
heavy, frangible, palpable.

But if you've still means to play it,
an eye will tell you as well as
an ear what's left, the cracked voices
brushing through white noise like shadows
on a curtain.   Something mortal
about shellac, you always know
where you are, a faint scratching
through reducing time that spirals
faster as it nears the centre's
horizon, until the soft black
repeating hiss of a circle
going nowhere, as circles do –
needle's voice whispering nothing –
announces the end, endlessly.